THREED, THIS ROAD NOT DAMASCUS

Threed, This Road Not Damascus

Poems by Tamara J. Madison

THP

Madison, Tamara J.
1st edition.

ISBN: 978-1-9494870-3-9
Library of Congress Control Number: 2018954475

Interior Layout & Cover Design by Lea C. Deschenes
Editing by Tayve Neese & Sara Lefsyk

Printed in Tennessee, USA
Trio House Press, Inc.
Ponte Vedra Beach, FL

To contact the author, send an email to tayveneese@gmail.com.

TABLE OF CONTENTS

ONE

TWO

THREE

In honor and loving memory of my foremothers...

"threed" - (adj.) having the quality of three or a trio of; carrying three breasts (or other appendage) where normally there are two; of or descending from beings of three breasts though the third has dissolved by way of devolution; powerfully compassionate beyond ordinary human behavior

- (n.) a being carrying three breasts (or another appendage) where normally there are two

- (n.) - a kin or descendant of one who is "threed"

ONE

In the beginning...

Genesis 1:1
(King James Version)

WOMBING: THREE-BREASTED WOMAN SHARES HER BIRTH STORY

... And in the 7th hour of the 8th day, the universe poured herself into herself, and I was born ripple of riveting wind, lotus in my left hand, machete long as I am tall in my right.

Upon my knees, I kissed and whispered Life into the womb of Death. He trembled in my protective arms bursting into droplets of Light.

Smiting lies with one righteous blow, I gathered the keening cries of moaning multitudes upon my back. I nursed them on goddess milk, swaddled them in sacred scrolls, raised them into shouts of jubilation and victory!

My own "I am" infinitely conceiving, I am she who swallowed the sun whole to birth bejeweled shadows.

Nowtime, millenniums after that 7th hour and 8th day, I long to lay my weapon down, dance with lotus in my hair and you in my embrace. I did not come here just to fight. I came to love you.

REBUTTAL: THREE-BREASTED WOMAN CONFRONTS KING JAMES I

Who can find a virtuous woman?
for her price is far above rubies.

Proverbs 31:10
(King James Version)

Really, James?
A virtuous woman, a price,
any woman, a price, a "piece,"
maid, trade, an enslaved,
wet nurse, cook, cunt, trophy, a price?

This life– damnation and dowry,
rubies, gold,
a dollar, pound, yen,
my hair, your glory,
my hips, the hills you climb
for the right price?

James, king almighty,
even your queen for a pence? Must you
buy everything?

BEATITUDES: THREE-BREASTED WOMAN'S SERMON ON THE MOUNT

Blessed: the breast
adorned with palm prints
pressed from hungry suckling,
the breast that hushes the baby,
soothes the "nuisance," quells the colic
(in private, never public, of course).
Better this formula, this powder, this chemical than your breast.

Oh, the black/brown/red/yellow breast drained by blue-eyed greed
    and pinked cheek!

Blessed: the sagging breast,
the nipple-to-the-knee, kiss-the-earth breast,
the perkiest breast, nipple tipped skyward
braving buffed sun and ripe wind.

Blessed: the siliconic breast,
bound and gagged,
stuffed and fluffed,
nipples rezoned,
the "might as well go ahead and remove it" breast
"because your mother and sister had cancer,
and you will probably have cancer too,"
the reconstructed breast ballooned,
nipples, areola tattooed.

Oh, the crone, maiden, MIA breast wreaking wrath and
    lamentation!

Blessed: the freed and flayed breast
valued, though never priceless

gracing magazine covers, centerfolds,
voguing on newsstands at street corners,
bursting through convenience stores, gas stations,
threatening the safety of the airport and freeways,
tempting the sanctity of bishops in their bulging pulpits.

Oh, the breast that garnishes "the industry" selling cunt, cars,
    cosmetics
(in public, never private, of course).

Blessed: the leprous breast
marred and decaying,
famished of cuddle/caress,
the breast sprinkled with landmines,
bearing boots of AWOL soldiers.

Oh, the breast that quells the hunger of a ravenous lover, paints
    throbbing blue balls blush!

Blessed: the breast waging protest,
keening, cradling the world in her capacitized cleavage!

Blessed be,
Blessed be,
Blessed be
the breast, threed!

Restraint: Three-Breasted Woman on the Auction Block

Awaiting the highest hungry bidder,
I dare not shudder.
These hunters thirst
blood, gut
of the innocent—
delectable delicacies for their
insanity insatiable.

My lack of symmetry amuses them.
They ponder a harness or snare
to fit, entangle these,
find me lush novelty,
freak-wonder to feed their foul fantasies.
Not enough hands, mouths, minds
to fondle, digest this.

Would it comfort, confound,
frighten them more
to know once upon a time
we all were threed?

Found Restitution: Maternal Lineage 1

for Malinda, Nancy, and Mary
(upon discovery of a court document from 1887)

Baker versus Calvert,
husband versus mistress,
master versus "former" enslaved, $30.00.

Inconspicuous the whip, shackles, and shanty,
a meager $30.00 finally settled the transfer of Master Baker's
    "property,"
the "property" also known as Malinda's children, Nancy and
    Mary, $30.00.

Emancipation Proclamation and DNA be damned.
Until jurisdiction and death did them part,
these $30.00-daughters called their father, "Mister Baker."

Juneteenth come and gone.
Forty acres and a mule
never sooned.

Prophecy: Maternal Lineage 2

for Malinda

On the back of the photograph,
one of my foremothers wrote,
"This is Malinda."
She knew one day
a century later
I would need to find you
framed in sepia,
statuesque and fierce, eyes
locked into the camera.
You long saw me coming.

Grandmama kept you hidden
fearing you'd blotch her milky skin, mar
her Christian countenance.
Uncle says you were Native,
corn-cob-pipe-smoking "indian."
Others say you, Moor,
descendant of the originals
who first tamed Turtle Island.
Textbooks and scripture twisted
your legacy into caricature.

I say, the way you stand there
in your Sunday-dressed best
staring across generations at me,
daring me to be free, Miss Malinda,
Madame, you were never anybody's slave.

Saint Ola

for Mama

"Unfit for the pulpit"
with Bible leather strapping your throat,
grosgrain tying your tongue, you,
they force fed,
broke your jaws and legs,
pried open your lips,
crammed their gospels into your mouths
until

drowning in waters Holy,
you joined the pantheon
of mistress martyrs baptized, evangelized
though never a mass, hymn or scripture
memorializing your name.

Luck of this Irish:
Maternal Lineage 3

By way of "Mr. Baker"
who never married but "took" Malinda,
(in the Biblical sense) begat
Nancy Iona who begat
Carlton Dulaney who begat
MariOla who begat
me, I-rich,
I am.
Nothing ado with Shamrock Soup
though corned beef and cabbage,
potatoes white and yammed always
staples in our homes.
No dandelion dreams,
though I have eaten dandelion greens,
worn their weedy blossoms in my nappy hair.
Kontomblé know my name, but
I have never seen a leprechaun, so
who is this, your Patrick?

TRINITIES: PATERNAL LINEAGE I

for Frances

Genesis:

three women

mother

sister   daughter

three mothers

'Sancey

'Cille   'Lois

three sons

James

Kenneth   Charles

three sir names

Madison

Higgs   Grundy

*

Exodus:

three women, three mothers, three sons

no sirs
no husbands
no fathers

*

Revelations:

their legacy, infinite

secrets

Poet's Arrival

Ripped the foreskin of my fathers' dreams.

Thrust from ragged wombs,
nursed on battered breasts,
whispered from my mothers' severed tongues,

here I come

blood rush, honed bone,
swaddled in thorny brine,
brimstone my bed.

My pillow, a pillar of salt.
My fathers' muffled moans,
my mothers' shrieking eyes—
my lullaby.

TRIBUNAL: PATERNAL LINEAGE 2

Uncle drank, tongued
the mouths of hard liquor bottles.
His fingers rummaged
ruffles of pastel panties,
plowed past their borders.
It was private
just between him and
two, three, four,
five... of them?

From across the room,
he sniffed his fingers,
licked their tendered pinkness,
grinned. Choked with shame,
they ran.

     *

SisBaby testified.
All the Grand and Auntie Mamas
caught whiff of that rife wind.
These Blood Hens
loosed their wings,
strutted their stuff.
Feathers and sparks flew.
Their cackles and curses
ripped the wet air,
strapped him to the chair.
Cluck and spit bound him tight.

They pecked that crooked grin right off his face.

The old cock cowered, fell limp.
No grin, no creep, no crow
no more.

The Queen's Libations

for MariOla

All the king's men have arrived.
Relations are gathered, Mama,
for the mourning fest
beholding your former body poised-
hair not grayed,
fingers straightened,
wrinkles smoothed, almost
a smile even now
to ease their pains.
Day of your body's
burial, I am raining
a new moon, sanguine libation
in honor of the life you chose,
tried to live.

Relations seen, unseen,
gathered watch

the man who
tried to love you
crack and crumble,
his grief oozing over
the metal that cradles
the emptied body.

The king's men cannot put him together again.

Your heart erupted,
ethereal shower to baptize us.
Your smile spit shines rainbows.
Dusk awaits your warmth while mosquitoes
hush their humming to hear

you sing.
I feel you
now, wild and rushing.

Twelve days, non-stop, Mama,
for you I pour this life tide-
wild, rushing ruby rain
to heal us all.

Contact: Poet Encounters Three-Breasted Woman

Following the queen's libations,
She appears
gradually taking shape
even before my blindness.
Her never blinking eyes
beckon me.
She anoints my sleep,
echoes my days,
reveals herself:
two-wombed, three-breasted,
dancing, laughing,
shackles at her hands and feet.
She sacrifices herself to chaos
that I be born.

Her familiar whispers confirm:
I will never be a motherless child.
I come from a long line of "threeds."

TWO

And he took bread, and gave thanks,
and brake it, and gave unto them, saying,
This is my body which is given for you:
this do in remembrance of me.

Luke 22:19
(King James Version)

Passover: Three-Breasted Woman Confronts King James 2

And though I break it,
my body, your bread,
give unto you whole grained,
firmly kneaded, fully risen,
buttered and plentiful,
the very prize of my harvest,
the bed of your belly,

you remember me not.

Manifesto: The Ten Commandments

I) Be a virgin.

At least appear pristine
though his hands be dirty.
He solicits purity.

"Wait until marriage."

II) Be alluring prey, prize of the hunt.

Act as though
you enjoy the chase.
He fiends, the rush.

"Don't call him.
Let him call you."

III) Feed him.

As you siphon droplets of soup
and ration crumbs
from pennies, your plate,
be prepared for his voracious appetite.

"Who wants a woman
who can't cook?"

IV) Be unaged though seasoned wine.

He requires beauty
for his drunken pleasures.
He can afford to age,
fatten, wrinkle, gray;
you cannot.

"Keep yourself up!"

V) Be sweet all ways, always.

He craves sweetness.
Should you become tart or bitter,
he will find his sweets someplace else,
gorge to the point of decay.

"No one likes a female boss,
butch, or bitch."

VI) Prepare for market crash.
He covets all
resources and wealth.
"Keep a secret bank account."

VII) Protect him.
Hide your menses and afterbirth.
It makes him squeamish,
reminds him of his mortality
and your power.
He desires omnipotence.
"Never let him know
you are on your period."

VIII) Worship him.
Handle your intellect, brilliance
with utmost modesty.
He craves dominion
over everything.
"Let him think
it was his idea."

IX) Feign fragility.
Manifest his destiny.
His masculinity always trumps
your femininity.
"Never emasculate him."

X) Be accountable.
Even when it is not your responsibility,
if you refuse such sacrifice,
the world will end.
"It's Eve's fault."

POET'S CONSUMMATION

for Kaba

Crashed the stone tablets of commandments,
their dust blown to higher winds.

I searched the darkest caves, made tombs my home,
deciphered the writings on the walls to find you.

Only in my stillness did you arrive.

At last, I offer my scarred wombs, my loosed tongues,
my asymmetry, my "threed" vision.

Beloved,
>   within me
>   there is no place
>   you may not enter.

ABINDIGO

for our son

You, conceived in fiery furnace,
your mama and daddy fanning
unrelenting flames.
Suddenly, my gate breaks.
Squat and she-wolf howling from a fence,
my hips, the pendulum, swing to reap you.
As your halo tumbles,
a cantata of wounded angels
bemoans your fretful fall.

The Physical

Her *sexe* giggles as
from her blushing labia
hundreds of bubbles leap and prance.
Like a child before a birthday camera,
her yoni grins before the doctor
as her knobby knees twitch,
curled toes and leanest limbs
flit in giddy girl-glory.

Suddenly, I and all the "threed" that ever were
lay our fury down and   weep.

Tongue Blade

for my daughter

Tempting seventeen,
you, woman-child,

the sweetest spin
in your mama's softest song,

lilt in her litany of love, you,
milken moon drizzled on parched night.

Your tongue lash? Our release:
your mothers' muted screams.

COVENANT

Daughter, War Goddess,
eyes, molasses pools fishing mine,
although you came ready-made,
know that I will pull the thread
from the very last horizon
and weave elegant mail to gird you.
I will melt stars,
hammer for hours your shield.

With these mouths of mine, I, ju woman,
will break bread of stone,
swallow the moon full,
drink a river rushing,
and sop blood with a biscuit for you.
With mortal arms and wilting fingers,
I will reach beyond the bowels of Time,
bring forth your sword.

Upon your dauntless victory,
Earth Daughter,
even as an old woman
ever pregnant with laughter,
surrounded by striplings,
showering seeds
upon my whirling garden,
I shall dance along the beach's edge
gathering shells and bones,
casting psalms upon the waters.

I shall dance along that beach's edge
in praise of glorious
you.

Wash Belly

for Afriel

I once flew
with the Angel
inside my belly,
his wings fluttering,
waves of amniotic sea.

Now we swim the abyss:
superheroes, our quest,
our nemeses, a thrill ride.

Runs in our tights, capeless,
girded with mammy-made gadgetry,
together we roam the streets of Gotham
raining kryptonite on lanternless nights—
his wings wilted, dusty,
my hair white, belly dry.

RAINDANCING

Wings tucked beneath fleece
hoodie, halo hidden in a Santa-red ski cap,
the Angel plays ball with raindrops
as the neighborhood boys envy,
their noses pressed to dripping panes.

Three weeks, 5 days, 7 hours,
since my last poem--
my muse on hiatus
in some other lover's lap
without as much as
a forwarding address or postcard.
I abandon pen and pad
to join the Angel, court raindrops,
flick my flip flops to the air,
ruffle my skirt in wetness,
cancan smack dab in the middle of a puddle,
baptizing the Angel with squeals and mud buttons.

I pull a moth-gnawed memory
from my left breast,
teach the Angel to spread his arms
until his chest aches,
turn his palms upward,
raise his face, close his eyes.
Suddenly, to the holy hum of cloud cum, home
my muse rushes
as wings ripping fleece,
the Angel opens his mouth to strain of cheek,
stretches out a perfectly curled tongue,
kisses rain.

POSTCARD

for my first born

Dear god,
I no longer seek your face.
I peeped it 20 years ago
wet from my leaking breast.
I miss you, long
to see you table dancing
on the altar of some esteemed cathedral
causing clergy to mess themselves
or maybe, god, turn liquor
into Living Water and crack
into some blindingly precious gemstone or
how about hitchhiking
along the Bible Belt Interstate
completely disrobing,
tuning rush hour?

Recently,
you whispered
your first name
felt, unspoken.
I simply can't remember
where I put it.

Focus: Poet Studies Three-Breasted Woman

I see her more clearly now.
Her skin, like the seasons, changes,
a myriad of earth tones
from bleached sands to blackest blues,
her hair, afroed sea foam
or lilting locks
glowing in the darkest abyss.
Through her one voice,
many tongues speak
though her lips never move.
Her eyes illuminate and pierce,
a gaze to birth or kill at will.
Though myth has yet to touch her,
she frequents my lucid dreams,
beckons me,
claims me,
prodigy.

ANTITHESIS: THREE-BREASTED WOMAN REBUKES KING JAMES

if it be a son, then ye shall kill him:
but if it be a daughter,
then she shall live.

Exodus 1:16
(King James Version)

And how might the daughters
live without the sons
except bemoan and suffer the horror
of your passionate perversion?

Debunk, defy, conjure!

HYPOTHESIS: POET QUESTIONS KING JAMES

God bleeds
through rivers and trees,
feathers, furs, and scales, concrete,
shimmers among the least of crystals. Perhaps
you kill
because you cannot find
your god
staring back in the mirror, or do
you kill
because you see God
when gazing at
me?

Vertigo Blues

chew you without
teeth melting muscle
blues juice steeped
pink tongue less
kiss taste places
i've missed kiss
please answer please

*

last night
panting in the fog
i kissed
her palm

    She wept

*

today
searching for my milk
i am but a nipple
of her breast
mastectomized
by unclean hands

*

flinching cringed
clenched in fist
this vertigo

Reproved

What woman think she not
muddied welcome mat,
broke-in bed-warmer,
Bartman, Leaks, D'Arc,
lit match beneath her feet?
From decorated throne to hearth of home,
banter of board/locker rooms,
in this place of breast unsafe--
bruise beneath baton
bleating rage and hatred,
noose dangling from the ribbons of "justice,"
knee anchored in her chest,
blade turning in her belly,
what woman think she not
keffired, niggered, muled?

PRECIPICE

pragmatic ecstatic
equatorial cool
the stony silence
lynched breaths
charming violence
the breached hope
bleached promise
stigmatic vision
the ill erotic
mundane exotic
intimate agnostic
licentious abstention
antiquated invention
stillbirthed rebirth...

before the nascent spring,
between us always
permeating our lives
the little deaths

Billboard

Newark, New Jersey

Instead of God's latest telegram or directions to the nearest
    gas and eats,
the billboard brazenly displays:

a face, a portrait
the eyes, two moons

a face, pixilated portrait
the eyes, two hollow moons, no stars

a face, pixilated portrait, a corpse in billboard casket
the eyes, two hollow, mute moons, no stars, no heaven to
    shroud them.

The billboard speaks above the city's streets,
"Unidentified victim. Please call 1-800… if you know him."

Any block, borough, mama out there, missing a face, this face,
    his
face? Any sun anywhere missing those two hollow, mute
    moons?

The pixilated portrait: his face, two moons, no stars, no
    heaven,
the billboard casket– a sinned city's saving grace interred.

Flora

For them noosed and strung
from your withering family tree,
catching searing razor or metallic seed
between jewels, teeth or spleen,
crosses aflame upon the scars of their backs--
with one blink of the sun,
stars shed their skins
instead of tears.
The sloughs slip
among the heavenly bodies,
drift on crippled winds, wriggle
through the whimpering willows' leaves,
land softly on a regiment
of weeds bending
to bear them as honors
before they slip again
to hardened soil yet fecund
with prophecy.

Titanium threads root,
silver stems ascend,
concrete contracts, splits
as copper waters birth
crowning heads
of cast iron roses.

Weaving

She loathes them.

Americans. Wishes she could find one.
Shred it to pieces to weave her mourning veil.

A horrid Black Hawk,
ripping her meager piece
of alkebulanian sky, hovered
to lay its poisonous eggs.

The village could not find enough
of her three-year old
to bury.

Her eyes twitch.
Her fingers twiddle.
The starving loom waits.

KASHOUSH

for Ibrahim

While many fondle their pens,
pimp, blaspheme the mic
with their faded blues and pop whoredom,
somewhere in nearby tragedy, others

butcher poets—

tie their tongues,
slit and peel their throats,
display their broken vocal chords
for public viewing.

But the immortal song of resistance
lingers on deadening silence
awaiting another birth,
another bard, prophet,
poet to wail and croon
another day come soon.

S.O.S.: Poet Appeals to Three-Breasted Woman

His head strewn, a leg here, an arm there, the torso in hideous pieces, phallus devoured...

What possessed you to search until you found every bit of him? How did you know you could put him back together, awaken him? Were you confident you would conceive? Was it your love that resurrected him?   Did you fear a monstrous mutation of the seed posthumous?

Forgive me the press for answers. Our lovers too, sisters, and sons are falling, our efforts futile.

What on earth will become of us?

Nativity: Three-Breasted Woman Anoints Poet

My song is recorded
in the very beat of your heart,
my wand beneath your pillow
as you dream.
Your keen conception,
my illuminating brilliance.
Let not their confliction
of your "matter"
confound you.

No history revised, treachery surmised
can extinguish this knighted nascence,
this native daughter, son.

INTERSTICE

Like the missing
breast, center-chest,
I am the between,
commuting realms,
one of the few who
hears, sees her, translates
her ancient, sacred tongue
into this language
primitive and secular.

With poem, deed,
though antigodlin,
I am yet "threed"
tilling and tending this
bludgeoned Eden.

Urban Powwow

the Women's Performance Workshop,
7 Stages Theater, Atlanta

Women with stories:
herstories, shestories, and goddess myths.
One-women, two-women,
red-women, blue-women,
loving women, hurting women,
seething, redeeming women
revenge-stained, fearless.

Women breathing for all the women
holding their breaths beneath
murderous thrusts of rage,
women with boots stomping their mouths
pummeled by flaming fists,
necks snapped by flick of savage wrists,
woman-breaths chewed, spat
back into their faces.

Breathing for all breaths dusted
with gunpowder, charred by bomb blasts,
gambled on surgery tables, breathing
for all breaths wrung dry
from every woman/man/child,
their pleas ignored.

Volcanic swells, our bodies,
breathing, purifying pyres.

Poet Conjures: Post-Mortem

"In 38 minutes of fear and chaos today, an unarmed woman
with a history of mental illness lead secret service and law
enforcement on a wild car chase. After ramming into the
barricade next to the White House and later circling the
peace monument, she was fatally shot without leaving her
driver's seat; the one-year old infant in the back seat survived.
A moment of silent prayer was held on the House floor for
the officers injured who feared for their lives and the safety of
others.

In other news, God committed suicide, his body found
dangling on a teepeed tree rooted in the White House lawn.
The locals surmised a lynching. Their suspicions remain
unmerited."

> While others fuel the frenzy,
> fodder for another kill,
> I bless and wash the feet of Time.
> Holy water dripping from my palms,
> I carefully collect broken souls,
> enough to plant a garden,
> from the bloodied soil,
> sculpt a woman.
> Between mantra, mojo, conjure,
> soon be over this mourning.

UN-INTERNMENT: THREE-BREASTED WOMAN ORDAINS POET

Injected with genocide,
you have swallowed
bomb, bullet, knife, lies
a thousand times.

Open your eyes. Rise.
Go and die
no more.

EASTER

Dewless grass, balding dogwoods,
limp lilies, sterile bunnies stuffed
with corner store chocolates and tattooed eggs.

How to explore new territory
when all I can see is the previously logged and charted:
remnants of ragged breasts,
swatches of tattered apron,
my feet swollen and bound
for dreams I am struggling to remember?
The spring of my life
compass rusted, needle arthritic,

my shoulder blue-black,
the bleeding stone to roll away.

CATECHISM: THREE-BREASTED WOMAN TEACHES

Foolish children ask me,

"Can you feed multitudes with loaves and fish,
convert water to wine, tip toe the sea?"

I stiffly hold my tongues thinking
the nations I shat, bushels I fried. Besides

who needs fish, wine, or floating feet
when threed across dimensions fly?

Nomenclature: Poet's Research I

Today, I learned
one of your many names
in an ancient tongue
translates as *the many breasted one.*

Many breasted...
and we attempt to confine you
to three simple letters,

many...
powder your face with ambiguity,
swear you muscle-chested, ductless, yet

we gluttonously suckle forgetting:

save the Breast,
save the world.

ANATOMY: POET'S RESEARCH 2

She : We

We : I

I : She

:

"threed"

POET'S TRANSCENDENCE

Finally, it's just us.
I lie in the crook
of your elbow
safe, brave,
enough
to become
smaller than small.
My skin
begins to effervesce
dancing coils
around your lifeline.
The incredible shrinking woman
peacefully surrenders.
This once lost, three-breasted daughter,
finally returning Home.

Poet Ascending

Gently, I remove my breasts,
hang their crumpling shells
on the arms of a rugged cross,
plant my yoni at its foot.
Wind whispers vespers
through the craters of my winding corpse
as flapping wings a murder
a hymnal sings.

Poet's Resurrection

Undaunted, no longer dangling bait or adornment,
my bruises now the sweetest, virgin tears, my tea,

a hearty string of serpent fangs, my belly beads,
I am freed from the clench of Adam's teeth!

The kiss of lightning makes my marrow hum,
bursts my bush to sweating flames.

I shade the sun, confess the moon,
curtsey my king or rip him open,

shave my lion bald, feast upon his roar,
leave him cleave his aching silence.

I dare to open my eyes as
my "threed" rise,

leak my cleavages' need to poet language
lush enough to sweep the knees of Jesus.

Toe whipping air,
I resuscitate wind.

This dance I do,
this dance.

THE ROAD NOT DAMASCUS

Upon my return to *She*,

burn my bones
beneath the never-weeping-tree,
sprinkle the ashes at its roots,
gather, my loved ones,
hold each other closer.

Husband, do tell them
I bore the glinting silver of my locks as bejeweled crown,
my lips painted, a Blues moan magenta,
my dimpled calabash, a Hottentot throne.
I shat nations amid barren and defiled legacies.

Sisters, gently remind them
I laughed at Lucifer's charms,
flirted with angels,
seduced even the dead with my wine.

Daughters, Sons,
rhythmic thunder robed in lightning,
sweating pearls of spring rain,
remind each other often,
tell my generations while laughing
beneath the never-weeping-tree:
we be "threed."

LEGACY

I give you no longer
my blood honey, my bone
to sip and gnaw, soothe. Yet

this scroll,
I leave

etched in bone pen,
blood-inked,
soul-pressed,
not of clergy or Dead Sea,
but triumvirate,
living prophecy.

Psalms: In Praise of Three-Breasted Woman

Let the words of my mouth
And the meditation of my heart...

Psalms 19:14
(King James Version)

Pleated air and etched lace of snowflakes, her regalia,
burnished brass, her skin.
Rising from throne of relentless unrest,
She curtsies
and plucks a bass
with her toes.

Recalcitrant dance of deified Promise,
She:
ribbonic melody,
bubonic baritone.
Quadruple double "D's"
make Mojo snap his fingers, itch
his sweating palms.

This soulful siren:
the Muses' muse,
her tongue betrothed
to bereavement
and breakthrough.
Her breath broke
turns brush stroke
on a canvas absent of dreams.

She
swallows city slick,
spits hymns salacious
giving birth to the birth
of Cool.

This goddess of split riff
carried Jive on her left hip,
bestowed upon his gimp her swagger
to cut the skin of night to breech dawn.

She
fashions cultures
with the twist of her wrist,
jiggle of her thigh,
bat of her eye.
Her off beat, on point,
her off key pops the lock
holding Nat Turner's vision.

She:
tourniquet to clench
bleeding of the Red Sea.

Bossa Nova searing her veins,
She:
endless scat of untamed sass, quintessential class
shattering the confines of malicious myth,
conductress of sanctified symphony—
reed ripping,
sax groaning,
drum grunting,
eucharistic funktastrophy consecrated
on an altar of Lazarus kisses.

This shaman of riff split
wets dry bones,
bids skulls to bloom eyes,
and awaken hungry
questing flesh again.

From between her knees,
apocalypses tumble
suckled on messianic milk,
Jezebel breast.

She:
hell birthed,
celestially conceived.
Lust of conquering kings,
envy of alabaster queens.

Behold her as *She* shines!

And we, "threed,"
her mighty descendants,
the boptized and funktified,
and call her

arise
blessed!

Acknowledgements

Many thanks to the editors who selected and published these works in the following journals, magazines, anthologies, and on-line publications:

"Psalms" first appeared as "The Christening" in *Ethel*, Fall 2018.

"S.O.S." and "Nativity" appear in *aaduna*, Winter/Spring 2016.

"Beatitudes" first appeared as "Ode to the Breast" in *aaduna*, Winter 2014.

"Luck of this Irish" appears in *Poetry International*, Issue #17.

"Tongue Blade" appears in *aaduna*, Fall 2012.

"Easter" appears in *Ellipsis*, Spring 2012.

"The Queen's Libations" first appeared as "Libations" in *Manzanita Quarterly*, Vol. 4, No. 4.

"Tribunal" appeared in part as "Blood Hens" in *Black Magnolias*, Spring 2011.

"Raindancing" appears in *Turbulence Magazine*, Issue #5, and in *Kentucky Curdled*.

"Poet's Resurrection" first appeared as "Undaunted" in *Henniker Review*, Spring 2011.

"Vertigo Blues" appears in *Henniker Review*, Spring 2011.

"Flora" originally appeared as "Not Just a Tupac Poem" in *Henniker Review*, Spring 2010.

"Covenant" first appeared as "Ajeemah's Psalm" in *Runes*, Winter 2007.

Gratitude

I am grateful to all my teachers and mentors including: poets Sterling D. Plumpp, Jeff Friedman, Paula McLain, Carol Frost, Ilya Kaminsky, and musician/composer, Kahil El'Zabar. My gratitude extends to Bill Berry, Jr. and my *aaduna* family for consistent love and artistic support and to Aquarius Press/ Willow Books for acknowledgement of the earlier form of this manuscript, *Breast Poems*, in the 2015 Willow Books Literature Awards. I am grateful also to my editors, Sara Lefsyk and Tayve Neese, and to Trio House Press for their commitment to publishing this work.

I am truly blessed and thankful for the host of family, friends, "sister circle," and community who share their stories with me, support, and encourage me on the toughest days. I also thank my students who keep me motivated and committed to my own growth. I extend very special thanks to my sister, children and partner who continuously and graciously share me with the page, stage, and classroom.

Finally, I offer my eternal gratitude to my mother who first infused my life with the arts and to my father who believed his daughters could do absolutely anything.

About the Book

Threed, This Road Not Damascus was designed at Trio House Press through the collaboration of:

Tayve Neese, Lead Editor
Sara Lefsyk, Supporting Editor
Lea C. Deschenes, Interior Design & Cover Design

The text is set in Adobe Caslon Pro.

The publication of this book is made possible, whole or in part, by the generous support of the following individuals and/or agencies:

Anonymous

About the Press

Trio House Press is a collective press. Individuals within our organization come together and are motivated by the primary shared goal of publishing distinct American voices in poetry. All THP published poets must agree to serve as Collective Members of the Trio House Press for twenty-four months after publication in order to assist with the press and bring more Trio books into print. Award winners and published poets must serve on one of four committees: Production and Design, Distribution and Sales, Educational Development, or Fundraising and Marketing. Our Collective Members reside in cities from New York to San Francisco.

Trio House Press adheres to and supports all ethical standards and guidelines outlined by the CLMP.

Trio House Press, Inc., is dedicated to the promotion of poetry as literary art, which enhances the human experience and its culture. We contribute in an innovative and distinct way to American Poetry by publishing emerging and established poets, providing educational materials, and fostering the artistic process of writing poetry. For further information, or to consider making a donation to Trio House Press, please visit us online at: www.triohousepress.org.

Other Trio House Press Books you might enjoy:

Two Towns Over by Darren C. Demaree
    2017 Trio Award Winner selected by Campbell McGrath

Bird~Brain by Matt Mauch, 2017

Dark Tussock Moth by Mary Cisper
    2016 Trio Award Winner selected by Bhisham Bherwani

Break the Habit by Tara Betts, 2016

Bone Music by Stephen Cramer
    2015 Louise Bogan Award selected by Kimiko Hahn

Rigging a Chevy into a Time Machine and Other Ways
    to Escape a Plague by Carolyn Hembree
    2015 Trio Award Winner selected by Neil Shepard

Magpies in the Valley of Oleanders by Kyle McCord, 2015

Your Immaculate Heart by Annmarie O'Connell, 2015

The Alchemy of My Mortal Form by Sandy Longhorn
    2014 Louise Bogan Winner selected by Carol Frost

What the Night Numbered by Bradford Tice
    2014 Trio Award Winner selected by Peter Campion

Flight of August by Lawrence Eby
    2013 Louise Bogan Winner selected by Joan Houlihan

The Consolations by John W. Evans
    2013 Trio Award Winner selected by Mihaela Moscaliuc

Fellow Odd Fellow by Steven Riel, 2013

Clay by David Groff
    2012 Louise Bogan Winner selected by Michael Waters

Gold Passage by Iris Jamahl Dunkle
    2012 Trio Award Winner selected by Ross Gay

If You're Lucky Is a Theory of Mine by Matt Mauch, 2012

CPSIA information can be obtained
at www.ICGtesting.com
Printed in the USA
FFHW020942190519
52552026-58004FF